hOUR BY hOUR

Forward Movement
412 Sycamore Street, Cincinnati, Ohio 45202-4195
800-543-1813
www.forwardmovement.org

Forward Movement, an official, non-profit agency of The Episcopal Church, is sustained through sales and tax-free contributions from our readers.

Preface

TIME. The spiritual tradition tells us that time is a creature (part of creation). Time is one of the things over which we have no control. It cannot be stopped or manipulated and it flows in only one direction—at least as far as we know. It can, however, be sanctified. The minutes, hours, days, months, and years are capable of being woven into a pattern of praise and penitence, giving shape to our joys and sorrows, tragedies and triumphs. It is a truism to say that time seems to be speeding up. What were thought to be great time savers are simply the means by which we cram more and more into our day. Some of us are addicted to velocity and stress. Time is running away with us.

This little book to help us pray the hours couldn't have come at a more important time. Human beings need a way to punctuate time at regular intervals. We eventually become what we pay attention to, what we contemplate; and paying attention to our hearts in their longing for God eventually builds us up as children of God, and brothers and sisters of each other. Reading daily verses of scripture, especially the psalms, provides the architecture of our thoughts and teaches us how to experience the world aright. Time becomes a friend instead of an enemy.

It has been said that there are only two prayers: Help! and Thank You! The rest are footnotes.

When I was growing up, we were told in Sunday school that the five elements of prayer are Adoration, Praise, Confession, Thanksgiving, and Supplication. This book of hours provides a structure of these five elements and two basic prayers. Adoration and Thanksgiving are primary. They place us in a right relationship with God and with all things. The poet, Mary Oliver, reminds us that the world offers itself to our imagination every day.

> *Whoever you are, no matter how lonely,*
> *the world offers itself to your imagination,*
> *calls you like the wild geese, harsh and exciting—*
> *over and over announcing your place*
> *in the family of things.*

I think this is one of the many things "the discipline of the daily office" gives us—a place in the family of creation.

Confession and Supplication are essential, too, because they are ways in which we practice self-examination and pray for others. The old way of thinking about confession was to call it "examination of conscience." I like to think of it as an examination of *consciousness*. I find it helpful to offer my mind (with all its busyness and noise) to God every day. Our consciousness with its fixations and obsessions needs cleansing and setting back on track. Beginning and ending the day with a brief time of reflection gives shape not only to the day but also to our life.

Being committed to a daily discipline of prayer which is common—shared and not merely private—puts us in touch with a great company of pilgrims through the ages and gives our life a healing rhythm—rather like the ground bass for the music of our lives.

Finally, you will find this little book eminently usable and even memorable. I would like to see the lost art of memorizing verses from scripture revived. They can become "arrow prayers" during the day to keep us focused and loving. And do not underestimate the power of prayer and the power of the prayers of a critical mass of faithful from all the great traditions holding the world together. It makes a difference. Using this book daily will deepen your commitment. It could even change your life. Carry it with you wherever you go. You won't regret it.

The Very Rev. Alan W. Jones
Dean of Grace Cathedral, San Francisco
Honorary Canon of the Cathedral of
Our Lady of Chartres

Introduction

The resources of *The Book of Common Prayer* are boundless. A single limitation is length—1001 pages—a large book, too big for pocket, handbag, even backpack.

The Book of Common Prayer, the book that unites Episcopalians, contains simple liturgy that makes it possible for each of us to offer prayer, hour by hour—morning, noon, evening, and compline—each day. Four of the daily office hours. A simple form of prayer, hour by hour, day by day.

Hour by Hour offers brief, liturgical material from *The Book of Common Prayer* enabling each one of us to say the hours: morning, noon, evening, compline. The lessons are taken from the New Revised Standard Version of the Bible.

Carry this book with you. Pray with it four times a day. Pray when you think of it. Pray even if you forget. This book is your hourly companion, your reminder that each one of us is a creature of God, a creature who lives and moves and has being, thanks to the God who creates and sustains us.

Sunday

Sunday

MORNING

Opening Sentence

This is the day which the Lord hath made; we will rejoice and be glad in it. *Psalm 118:24*

Canticle — *Venite*

Come, let us sing to the Lord; *
  let us shout for joy to the Rock of our salvation.
Let us come before his presence with thanksgiving *
  and raise a loud shout to him with psalms.

For the Lord is a great God, *
  and a great King above all gods.
In his hand are the caverns of the earth, *
  and the heights of the hills are his also.
The sea is his, for he made it, *
  and his hands have molded the dry land.

Come, let us bow down, and bend the knee, *
  and kneel before the Lord our Maker.
For he is our God,
and we are the people of his pasture and the sheep
                                  of his hand. *
  Oh, that today you would harken to his voice!

Glory to the Father, and to the Son, and to the Holy Spirit: *
   as it was in the beginning, is now, and will be for ever.
                                                    Amen.

Psalm 62

For God alone my soul in silence waits; *
   from him comes my salvation.

He alone is my rock and my salvation, *
   my stronghold, so that I shall not be greatly shaken.

How long will you assail me to crush me,
all of you together, *
   as if you were a leaning fence, a toppling wall?

They seek only to bring me down from my place
                              of honor; *
   lies are their chief delight.

They bless with their lips, *
   but in their hearts they curse.

For God alone my soul in silence waits; *
   truly, my hope is in him.

He alone is my rock and my salvation, *
   my stronghold, so that I shall not be shaken.

In God is my safety and my honor; *
   God is my strong rock and my refuge.

Put your trust in him always, O people, *
   pour out your hearts before him,
                        for God is our refuge.

Those of high degree are but a fleeting breath, *
   even those of low estate cannot be trusted.

On the scales they are lighter than a breath, *
   all of them together.

Put no trust in extortion;
in robbery take no empty pride; *
   though wealth increase, set not your heart
                        upon it.

God has spoken once, twice have I heard it, *
   that power belongs to God.

Steadfast love is yours, O Lord, *
   for you repay everyone according to his deeds.

Lesson

For the love of Christ urges us on, because we are
convinced that one has died for all; therefore all have
died. And he died for all, so that those who live might
live no longer for themselves, but for him who died
and was raised for them. *2 Corinthians 5:14-15*

 # The Lord's Prayer

Our Father, who art in heaven,
hallowed be thy Name,
thy kingdom come,
thy will be done,
on earth as it is in heaven.
Give us this day our daily bread.
And forgive us our trespasses,
as we forgive those
who trespass against us.
And lead us not into temptation,
but deliver us from evil.
For thine is the kingdom,
and the power, and the glory,
for ever and ever. Amen.

Collect

O God, you make us glad with the weekly remembrance of the glorious resurrection of your Son our Lord: Give us this day such blessing through our worship of you, that the week to come may be spent in your favor; through Jesus Christ our Lord. *Amen.*

Grace

The grace of our Lord Jesus Christ, and the love of God, and the fellowship of the Holy Spirit, be with us all evermore. *Amen.*

Sunday

NOON

Opening Sentence

O God, make speed to save us.
O Lord, make haste to help us.

Hymn

O God, creation's secret force,
Yourself unmoved, all motion's source,
You from the morn till evening's ray,
Through all its changes guide the day.

Psalm 119:105-108

Your word is a lantern to my feet *
    and a light upon my path.

I have sworn and am determined *
    to keep your righteous judgments.

I am deeply troubled; *

    preserve my life, O Lord, according to your word.

Accept, O Lord, the willing tribute of my lips, *

    and teach me your judgments.

Lesson

The love of God has been poured into our hearts through the Holy Spirit that has been given to us. *Romans 5:5*

 # The Lord's Prayer

    Our Father, who art in heaven,

        hallowed be thy Name,

        thy kingdom come,

        thy will be done,

            on earth as it is in heaven.

    Give us this day our daily bread.

    And forgive us our trespasses,

        as we forgive those

            who trespass against us.

    And lead us not into temptation,

        but deliver us from evil.

    For thine is the kingdom,

        and the power, and the glory,

        for ever and ever. Amen.

Thanksgiving

Accept, O Lord, our thanks and praise for all that you have done for us. We thank you for the splendor of the whole creation, for the beauty of this world, for the wonder of life, and for the mystery of love.

Grace

Let us bless the Lord.
Thanks be to God.

EVENING

Opening Sentence

Let my prayer be set forth in your sight as incense, the lifting up of my hands as the evening sacrifice.
Psalm 141:2

Canticle — *The Song of Mary*

My soul proclaims the greatness of the Lord,
my spirit rejoices in God my Savior; *
    for he has looked with favor on his lowly servant.

From this day all generations will call me blessed: *
    the Almighty has done great things for me,
    and holy is his Name.
He has mercy on those who fear him *
    in every generation.
He has shown the strength of his arm, *
    he has scattered the proud in their conceit.
He has cast down the mighty from their thrones, *
    and has lifted up the lowly.
He has filled the hungry with good things, *
    and the rich he has sent away empty.
He has come to the help of his servant Israel, *
    for he has remembered his promise of mercy,
The promise he made to our fathers, *
    to Abraham and his children for ever.

*Glory to the Father, and to the Son, and to the Holy Spirit: *
    as it was in the beginning, is now, and will be for ever.*
                              Amen.

Psalm 85:7-13

Show us your mercy, O LORD, *
    and grant us your salvation.

I will listen to what the LORD God is saying, *
    for he is speaking peace to his faithful people
    and to those who turn their hearts to him.

Truly, his salvation is very near to those who
fear him, *
that his glory may dwell in our land.

Mercy and truth have met together; *
righteousness and peace have kissed each other.

Truth shall spring up from the earth, *
and righteousness shall look down from heaven.

The LORD will indeed grant prosperity, *
and our land will yield its increase.

Righteousness shall go before him, *
and peace shall be a pathway for his feet.

Lesson

Blessed be the God and Father of our Lord Jesus
Christ, the Father of mercies and the God of all
consolation, who consoles us in all our affliction, so
that we may be able to console those who are in any
affliction with the consolation with which we ourselves are consoled by God. *2 Corinthians 1:3-4*

✤ The Lord's Prayer

Our Father, who art in heaven,
hallowed be thy Name,
thy kingdom come,
thy will be done,
on earth as it is in heaven.

Give us this day our daily bread.
And forgive us our trespasses,
as we forgive those
who trespass against us.
And lead us not into temptation,
but deliver us from evil.
For thine is the kingdom,
and the power, and the glory,
for ever and ever. Amen.

Collect

Lord God, whose Son our Savior Jesus Christ triumphed over the powers of death and prepared for us our place in the new Jerusalem: Grant that we, who have this day given thanks for his resurrection, may praise you in that City of which he is the light, and where he lives and reigns for ever and ever. *Amen.*

Grace

The grace of our Lord Jesus Christ, and the love of God, and the fellowship of the Holy Spirit, be with us all evermore. *Amen.*

Sunday
COMPLINE

Opening Sentence
The Lord Almighty grant us a peaceful night and a perfect end. *Amen.*

Psalm 4
Answer me when I call, O God, defender of
        my cause; *
  you set me free when I am hard-pressed;
  have mercy on me and hear my prayer.

"You mortals, how long will you dishonor
        my glory? *
  how long will you worship dumb idols
  and run after false gods?"

Know that the LORD does wonders for the faithful; *
  when I call upon the LORD, he will hear me.

Tremble, then, and do not sin; *
  speak to your heart in silence upon your bed.

Offer the appointed sacrifices *
  and put your trust in the LORD.

Many are saying,
"Oh, that we might see better times!" *
  Lift up the light of your countenance
              upon us, O Lord.

You have put gladness in my heart,
  more than when grain and wine and oil increase.

I lie down in peace; at once I fall asleep; *
  for only you, Lord, make me dwell in safety.

Lesson

Yet you, O Lord, are in the midst of us, and we
are called by your Name; do not forsake us!
Jeremiah 14:9

 ## The Lord's Prayer

Our Father, who art in heaven,
  hallowed be thy Name,
  thy kingdom come,
  thy will be done,
      on earth as it is in heaven.
Give us this day our daily bread.
And forgive us our trespasses,
  as we forgive those
      who trespass against us.

And lead us not into temptation,
but deliver us from evil.
For thine is the kingdom,
and the power, and the glory,
for ever and ever. Amen.

Collect

Be our light in the darkness, O Lord, and in your great mercy defend us from all perils and dangers of this night; for the love of your only Son, our Savior Jesus Christ. *Amen.*

Antiphon

Guide us waking, O Lord, and guard us sleeping; that awake we may watch with Christ, and asleep we may rest in peace.

Canticle — *The Song of Simeon*

Lord, you now have set your servant free *
    to go in peace as you have promised;
For these eyes of mine have seen the Savior, *
    whom you have prepared for all the world to see:
A Light to enlighten the nations, *
    and the glory of your people Israel.

Glory to the Father, and to the Son, and to the Holy Spirit: *
as it was in the beginning, is now, and will be for ever.
Amen.

Antiphon

Guide us waking, O Lord, and guard us sleeping;
that awake we may watch with Christ, and asleep
we may rest in peace.

Grace

The almighty and merciful Lord, Father, Son, and
Holy Spirit, bless us and keep us. *Amen.*

Monday

Monday
MORNING

Opening Sentence

Thanks be to God, which giveth us the victory
through our Lord Jesus Christ. *1 Corinthians 15:57*

Canticle — *Jubilate*

Be joyful in the Lord, all you lands; *
    serve the Lord with gladness
    and come before his presence with a song.

Know this: The Lord himself is God; *
    he himself has made us, and we are his;
    we are his people and the sheep of his pasture.

Enter his gates with thanksgiving;
go into his courts with praise; *
    give thanks to him and call upon his Name.

For the Lord is good;
his mercy is everlasting; *
    and his faithfulness endures from age to age.

*Glory to the Father, and to the Son, and to the Holy Spirit: ***
    as it was in the beginning, is now, and will be for ever.
Amen.

Psalm 1

Happy are they who have not walked in the
                    counsel of the wicked, *
    nor lingered in the way of sinners,
    nor sat in the seats of the scornful!

Their delight is in the law of the LORD, *
    and they meditate on his law day and night.

They are like trees planted by streams of water,
bearing fruit in due season, with leaves that do
                    not wither; *
    everything they do shall prosper.

It is not so with the wicked; *
    they are like chaff which the wind blows away.

Therefore the wicked shall not stand upright when
                    judgment comes, *
    nor the sinner in the council of the righteous.

For the LORD knows the way of the righteous, *
    but the way of the wicked is doomed.

Lesson

The night is far gone, the day is near. Let us then lay
aside the works of darkness and put on the armor of
light. *Romans 13:12*

 # The Lord's Prayer

Our Father, who art in heaven,
*   hallowed be thy Name,*
*   thy kingdom come,*
*   thy will be done,*
*   on earth as it is in heaven.*
Give us this day our daily bread.
And forgive us our trespasses,
*   as we forgive those*
*   who trespass against us.*
And lead us not into temptation,
*   but deliver us from evil.*
For thine is the kingdom,
*   and the power, and the glory,*
*   for ever and ever.* Amen.

Collect

O God, the King eternal, whose light divides the day from the night and turns the shadow of death into the morning: Drive far from us all wrong desires, incline our hearts to keep your law, and guide our feet into the way of peace; that, having done your will with cheerfulness during the day, we may, when night comes, rejoice to give you thanks; through Jesus Christ our Lord. *Amen.*

Grace

May the God of hope fill us with all joy and peace in believing through the power of the Holy Spirit. *Amen.*

Monday
NOON

Opening Sentence

O God, make speed to save us.
O Lord, make haste to help us.

Hymn

The golden sun lights up the sky,
Imparting vigor to the day.
Amid our customary round,
We offer you our prayer and praise.

Psalm 121

I lift up my eyes to the hills; *
   from where is my help to come?

My help comes from the LORD, *
   the maker of heaven and earth.

He will not let your foot be moved *
   and he who watches over you will not fall asleep.

Behold, he who keeps watch over Israel *
    shall neither slumber nor sleep;

The LORD himself watches over you; *
    the LORD is your shade at your right hand,

So that the sun shall not strike you by day, *
    nor the moon by night.

The LORD shall preserve you from all evil; *
    it is he who shall keep you safe.

The LORD shall watch over your going out and
                    your coming in, *
    from this time forth for evermore.

Lesson

So if anyone is in Christ, there is a new creation: everything old has passed away; see, everything has become new! All this is from God, who reconciled us to himself through Christ, and has given us the ministry of reconciliation. *2 Corinthians 5:17-18*

The Lord's Prayer

Our Father, who art in heaven,
    hallowed be thy Name,
    thy kingdom come,
    thy will be done,
        on earth as it is in heaven.
    Give us this day our daily bread.

And forgive us our trespasses,
    as we forgive those
        who trespass against us.
And lead us not into temptation,
    but deliver us from evil.
For thine is the kingdom,
    and the power, and the glory,
        for ever and ever. Amen.

Thanksgiving

We thank you for the blessing of family and friends, and for the loving care which surrounds us on every side.

Grace

Let us bless the Lord.
Thanks be to God.

Monday
EVENING

Opening Sentence

Grace to you and peace from God our Father and from the Lord Jesus Christ. *Philippians 1:2*

Canticle — *The Song of Mary*

My soul proclaims the greatness of the Lord,
my spirit rejoices in God my Savior; *
    for he has looked with favor on his lowly servant.
From this day all generations will call me blessed: *
    the Almighty has done great things for me,
    and holy is his Name.
He has mercy on those who fear him *
    in every generation.
He has shown the strength of his arm, *
    he has scattered the proud in their conceit.
He has cast down the mighty from their thrones, *
    and has lifted up the lowly.
He has filled the hungry with good things, *
    and the rich he has sent away empty.
He has come to the help of his servant Israel, *
    for he has remembered his promise of mercy,
The promise he made to our fathers, *
    to Abraham and his children for ever.

*Glory to the Father, and to the Son, and to the Holy Spirit: ***
    as it was in the beginning, is now, and will be for ever.
Amen.

Psalm 26

Give judgment for me, O Lord,
for I have lived with integrity; *
    I have trusted in the Lord and have not faltered.

Test me, O LORD, and try me; *
    examine my heart and my mind.

For your love is before my eyes; *
    I have walked faithfully with you.

I have not sat with the worthless, *
    nor do I consort with the deceitful.

I have hated the company of evildoers; *
    I will not sit down with the wicked.

I will wash my hands in innocence, O LORD, *
    that I may go in procession round your altar,

Singing aloud a song of thanksgiving *
    and recounting all your wonderful deeds.

LORD, I love the house in which you dwell *
    and the place where your glory abides.

Do not sweep me away with sinners, *
    nor my life with those who thirst for blood,

Whose hands are full of evil plots, *
    and their right hand full of bribes.

As for me, I will live with integrity; *
    redeem me, O LORD, and have pity on me.

My foot stands on level ground; *
    in the full assembly I will bless the LORD.

Lesson

Likewise the Spirit helps us in our weakness; for we do not know how to pray as we ought, but that very Spirit intercedes with sighs too deep for words. And God, who searches the heart, knows what is the mind of the Spirit, because the Spirit intercedes for the saints according to the will of God. We know that all things work together for good for those who love God, who are called according to his purpose. *Romans 8:26-28*

 ## The Lord's Prayer

Our Father, who art in heaven,
hallowed be thy Name,
thy kingdom come,
thy will be done,
on earth as it is in heaven.
Give us this day our daily bread.
And forgive us our trespasses,
as we forgive those
who trespass against us.
And lead us not into temptation,
but deliver us from evil.
For thine is the kingdom,
and the power, and the glory,
for ever and ever. Amen.

Collect

Most holy God, the source of all good desires, all right judgments, and all just works: Give to us, your servants, that peace which the world cannot give, so that our minds may be fixed on the doing of your will, and that we, being delivered from the fear of all enemies, may live in peace and quietness; through the mercies of Christ Jesus our Savior. *Amen.*

Grace

May the God of hope fill us with all joy and peace in believing through the power of the Holy Spirit. *Amen.*

COMPLINE

Opening Sentence

The Lord Almighty grant us a peaceful night and a perfect end. *Amen.*

Psalm 31

In you, O Lord, have I taken refuge;
let me never be put to shame: *
   deliver me in your righteousness.

Incline your ear to me; *
   make haste to deliver me.

Be my strong rock, a castle to keep me safe,
for you are my crag and my stronghold; *
   for the sake of your Name, lead me and guide me.

Take me out of the net that they have secretly set
               for me, *
   for you are my tower of strength.

Into your hands I commend my spirit, *
   for you have redeemed me,
   O Lord, O God of truth.

Lesson

"Come to me, all you that are weary and are carrying heavy burdens, and I will give you rest. Take my
yoke upon you, and learn from me; for I am gentle
and humble in heart, and you will find rest for your
souls. For my yoke is easy, and my burden is light."
Matthew 11:28-30

 # The Lord's Prayer

Our Father, who art in heaven,
hallowed be thy Name,
thy kingdom come,
thy will be done,
on earth as it is in heaven.
Give us this day our daily bread.
And forgive us our trespasses,
as we forgive those
who trespass against us.
And lead us not into temptation,
but deliver us from evil.
For thine is the kingdom,
and the power, and the glory,
for ever and ever. Amen.

Collect

Be present, O merciful God, and protect us through the hours of this night, so that we who are wearied by the changes and chances of this life may rest in your eternal changelessness; through Jesus Christ our Lord. *Amen.*

Antiphon

Guide us waking, O Lord, and guard us sleeping; that awake we may watch with Christ, and asleep we may rest in peace.

Canticle — *The Song of Simeon*

Lord, you now have set your servant free *
    to go in peace as you have promised;
For these eyes of mine have seen the Savior, *
    whom you have prepared for all the world to see:
A Light to enlighten the nations, *
    and the glory of your people Israel.

*Glory to the Father, and to the Son, and to the Holy Spirit: ***
    as it was in the beginning, is now, and will be for ever.
                                        Amen.

Antiphon

Guide us waking, O Lord, and guard us sleeping;
that awake we may watch with Christ, and asleep
we may rest in peace.

Grace

The almighty and merciful Lord, Father, Son, and
Holy Spirit, bless us and keep us. *Amen.*

Tuesday

MORNING

Opening Sentence

If then you have been raised with Christ, seek the things that are above, where Christ is, seated at the right hand of God. *Colossians 3:1*

Canticle — *The First Song of Isaiah*

Surely, it is God who saves me; *
    I will trust in him and not be afraid.
For the Lord is my stronghold and my sure defense,*
    and he will be my Savior.
Therefore you shall draw water with rejoicing *
    from the springs of salvation.
And on that day you shall say, *
    Give thanks to the Lord and call upon his Name;
Make his deeds known among the peoples; *
    see that they remember that his Name is exalted.
Sing the praises of the Lord, for he has done
                great things, *
    and this is known in all the world.
Cry aloud, inhabitants of Zion, ring out your joy, *
    for the great one in the midst of you is the
                Holy One of Israel.

*Glory to the Father, and to the Son, and to the Holy Spirit: ***
as it was in the beginning, is now, and will be for ever.
Amen.

Psalm 23

The LORD is my shepherd; *
  I shall not want.

He maketh me to lie down in green pastures; *
  he leadeth me beside the still waters.

He restoreth my soul; *
  he leadeth me in the paths of righteousness for
                  his Name's sake.

Yea, though I walk through the valley of the
                  shadow of death,
I will fear no evil; *
  for thou art with me;
  thy rod and thy staff, they comfort me.

Thou preparest a table before me in the presence
                  of mine enemies; *
  thou anointest my head with oil;
  my cup runneth over.

Surely goodness and mercy shall follow me all the
                  days of my life, *
  and I will dwell in the house of the LORD for ever.

King James Version

Lesson

But you, beloved, are not in darkness, for that day to surprise you like a thief; for you are all children of light and children of the day; we are not of the night or of darkness. *1 Thessalonians 5:4-5*

The Lord's Prayer

Our Father, who art in heaven,
hallowed be thy Name,
thy kingdom come,
thy will be done,
on earth as it is in heaven.
Give us this day our daily bread.
And forgive us our trespasses,
as we forgive those
who trespass against us.
And lead us not into temptation,
but deliver us from evil.
For thine is the kingdom,
and the power, and the glory,
for ever and ever. Amen.

Collect

O God, the author of peace and lover of concord, to know you is eternal life and to serve you is perfect freedom: Defend us, your humble servants, in all assaults of our enemies; that we, surely trusting in your defense, may not fear the power of any adversaries; through the might of Jesus Christ our Lord. *Amen.*

Grace

Glory to God whose power, working in us, can do infinitely more than we can ask or imagine: Glory to him from generation to generation in the Church, and in Christ Jesus for ever and ever. *Amen.*

NOON

Opening Sentence

O God, make speed to save us.
O Lord, make haste to help us.

Hymn

At the third hour you took your cross,
You stumbled, Lord, beneath its weight.
Now help us bear our daily load
And strive to follow where you lead.

Psalm 126

When the Lord restored the fortunes of Zion, *
   then were we like those who dream.

Then was our mouth filled with laughter, *
   and our tongue with shouts of joy.

They said among the nations, *
   "The Lord has done great things for them."

The Lord has done great things for us, *
   and we are glad indeed.

Restore our fortunes, O Lord, *
   like the watercourses of the Negev.

Those who sowed with tears *
   will reap with songs of joy.

Those who go out weeping, carrying the seed, *
   will come again with joy, shouldering their sheaves.

Lesson

For from the rising of the sun to its setting my name
is great among the nations, and in every place incense
is offered to my name, and a pure offering; for my
name is great among the nations, says the Lord of
hosts. *Malachi 1:11*

 # The Lord's Prayer

Our Father, who art in heaven,
hallowed be thy Name,
thy kingdom come,
thy will be done,
on earth as it is in heaven.
Give us this day our daily bread.
And forgive us our trespasses,
as we forgive those
who trespass against us.
And lead us not into temptation,
but deliver us from evil.
For thine is the kingdom,
and the power, and the glory,
for ever and ever. Amen.

Thanksgiving

We thank you for setting us at tasks which demand our best efforts, and for leading us to accomplishments which satisfy and delight us.

Grace

Let us bless the Lord.
Thanks be to God.

Tuesday
EVENING

Opening Sentence

Worship the Lord in the beauty of holiness; let the whole earth tremble before him. *Psalm 96:9*

Canticle — *The Song of Mary*

My soul proclaims the greatness of the Lord,
my spirit rejoices in God my Savior; *
    for he has looked with favor on his lowly servant.
From this day all generations will call me blessed: *
    the Almighty has done great things for me,
    and holy is his Name.
He has mercy on those who fear him *
    in every generation.
He has shown the strength of his arm, *
    he has scattered the proud in their conceit.
He has cast down the mighty from their thrones, *
    and has lifted up the lowly.
He has filled the hungry with good things, *
    and the rich he has sent away empty.
He has come to the help of his servant Israel, *
    for he has remembered his promise of mercy,
The promise he made to our fathers, *
    to Abraham and his children for ever.

Glory to the Father, and to the Son, and to the Holy Spirit: *
as it was in the beginning, is now, and will be for ever.
Amen.

Psalm 26:6-12

I will wash my hands in innocence, O LORD, *
that I may go in procession round your altar,

Singing aloud a song of thanksgiving *
and recounting all your wonderful deeds.

LORD, I love the house in which you dwell *
and the place where your glory abides.

Do not sweep me away with sinners, *
nor my life with those who thirst for blood,

Whose hands are full of evil plots, *
and their right hand full of bribes.

As for me, I will live with integrity; *
redeem me, O LORD, and have pity on me.

My foot stands on level ground; *
in the full assembly I will bless the LORD.

Lesson

Let love be genuine; hate what is evil, hold fast to what is good; love one another with mutual affection; outdo one another in showing honor. Do not lag in zeal, be ardent in spirit, serve the Lord. Rejoice in hope, be patient in suffering, persevere in prayer. *Romans 12:9-12*

✤ The Lord's Prayer

Our Father, who art in heaven,
hallowed be thy Name,
thy kingdom come,
thy will be done,
on earth as it is in heaven.
Give us this day our daily bread.
And forgive us our trespasses,
as we forgive those
who trespass against us.
And lead us not into temptation,
but deliver us from evil.
For thine is the kingdom,
and the power, and the glory,
for ever and ever. Amen.

Collect

Be our light in the darkness, O Lord, and in your great mercy defend us from all perils and dangers of this night; for the love of your only Son, our Savior Jesus Christ. *Amen.*

Grace

Glory to God whose power, working in us, can do infinitely more than we can ask or imagine: Glory to him from generation to generation in the Church, and in Christ Jesus for ever and ever. *Amen.*

Tuesday

COMPLINE

Opening Sentence

The Lord Almighty grant us a peaceful night and a perfect end. *Amen.*

Psalm 91

He who dwells in the shelter of the Most High *
    abides under the shadow of the Almighty.

He shall say to the Lord,
"You are my refuge and my stronghold, *
    my God in whom I put my trust."

He shall deliver you from the snare of the hunter *
    and from the deadly pestilence.

He shall cover you with his pinions,
and you shall find refuge under his wings; *
    his faithfulness shall be a shield and buckler.

You shall not be afraid of any terror by night, *
    nor of the arrow that flies by day;

Of the plague that stalks in the darkness, *
    nor of the sickness that lays waste at mid-day.

A thousand shall fall at your side
and ten thousand at your right hand, *
    but it shall not come near you.

Your eyes have only to behold *
    to see the reward of the wicked.

Because you have made the LORD your refuge, *
    and the Most High your habitation,

There shall no evil happen to you, *
    neither shall any plague come near your dwelling.

For he shall give his angels charge over you, *
    to keep you in all your ways.

They shall bear you in their hands, *
    lest you dash your foot against a stone.

You shall tread upon the lion and adder; *
    you shall trample the young lion and the
                            serpent under your feet.

Because he is bound to me in love,
therefore will I deliver him; *
    I will protect him, because he knows my Name.

He shall call upon me, and I will answer him; *
    I am with him in trouble;
    I will rescue him and bring him to honor.

With long life will I satisfy him, *
    and show him my salvation.

Lesson

Now may the God of peace, who brought back from the dead our Lord Jesus, the great shepherd of the sheep, by the blood of the eternal covenant, make you complete in everything good so that you may do his will, working among us that which is pleasing in his sight, through Jesus Christ, to whom be the glory forever and ever. Amen. *Hebrews 13:20-21*

 # The Lord's Prayer

Our Father, who art in heaven,
hallowed be thy Name,
thy kingdom come,
thy will be done,
on earth as it is in heaven.
Give us this day our daily bread.
And forgive us our trespasses,
as we forgive those
who trespass against us.
And lead us not into temptation,
but deliver us from evil.
For thine is the kingdom,
and the power, and the glory,
for ever and ever. Amen.

Collect

Look down, O Lord, from your heavenly throne, and illumine this night with your celestial brightness; that by night as by day your people may glorify your holy Name; through Jesus Christ our Lord. *Amen.*

Antiphon

Guide us waking, O Lord, and guard us sleeping; that awake we may watch with Christ, and asleep we may rest in peace.

Canticle — *The Song of Simeon*

Lord, you now have set your servant free *
    to go in peace as you have promised;
For these eyes of mine have seen the Savior, *
    whom you have prepared for all the world to see:
A Light to enlighten the nations, *
    and the glory of your people Israel.

*Glory to the Father, and to the Son, and to the Holy Spirit: **
    as it was in the beginning, is now, and will be for ever.
                Amen.

Antiphon

Guide us waking, O Lord, and guard us sleeping; that awake we may watch with Christ, and asleep we may rest in peace.

Grace

The almighty and merciful Lord, Father, Son, and Holy Spirit, bless us and keep us. *Amen.*

Wednesday

Wednesday
MORNING

Opening Sentence

If we say we have no sin, we deceive ourselves, and the truth is not in us, but if we confess our sins, God, who is faithful and just, will forgive our sins and cleanse us from all unrighteousness. *1 John 1:8-9*

Canticle — *The Second Song of Isaiah*

Seek the Lord while he wills to be found; *
    call upon him when he draws near.
Let the wicked forsake their ways *
    and the evil ones their thoughts;
And let them turn to the Lord, and he will have
                 compassion, *
    and to our God, for he will richly pardon.
For my thoughts are not your thoughts, *
    nor your ways my ways, says the Lord.
For as the heavens are higher than the earth, *
    so are my ways higher than your ways,
    and my thoughts than your thoughts.
For as rain and snow fall from the heavens *
    and return not again, but water the earth,
Bringing forth life and giving growth, *
    seed for sowing and bread for eating,

So is my word that goes forth from my mouth; *
   it will not return to me empty;
But it will accomplish that which I have purposed, *
   and prosper in that for which I sent it.

*Glory to the Father, and to the Son, and to the Holy Spirit: **
   as it was in the beginning, is now, and will be for ever.
                                                    Amen.

Psalm 46:1-8

God is our hope and strength, *
   a very present help in trouble.

Therefore will we not fear, though the earth be
                        moved, *
   and though the hills be carried into the midst
                        of the sea;

Though the waters thereof rage and swell, *
   and though the mountains shake at the tempest
                        of the same.

There is a river, the streams whereof make glad the
                        city of God, *
   the holy place of the tabernacle of the Most
                        Highest.

God is in the midst of her,
therefore shall she not be removed; *
   God shall help her, and that right early.

Be still then, and know that I am God; *
    I will be exalted among the nations,
    and I will be exalted in the earth.

The LORD of hosts is with us; *
    the God of Jacob is our refuge.

Lesson

Long ago God spoke to our ancestors in many and various ways by the prophets, but in these last days he has spoken to us by a Son, whom he appointed heir of all things, through whom he also created the worlds. *Hebrews 1:1-2*

✛ The Lord's Prayer

Our Father, who art in heaven,
    hallowed be thy Name,
    thy kingdom come,
    thy will be done,
        on earth as it is in heaven.
Give us this day our daily bread.
And forgive us our trespasses,
    as we forgive those
        who trespass against us.
And lead us not into temptation,
    but deliver us from evil.

For thine is the kingdom,
and the power, and the glory,
for ever and ever. Amen.

Collect

Lord God, almighty and everlasting Father, you have brought us in safety to this new day: Preserve us with your mighty power, that we may not fall into sin, nor be overcome by adversity; and in all we do, direct us to the fulfilling of your purpose; through Jesus Christ our Lord. *Amen.*

Grace

The grace of our Lord Jesus Christ, and the love of God, and the fellowship of the Holy Spirit, be with us all evermore. *Amen.*

NOON

Opening Sentence

O God, make speed to save us.
O Lord, make haste to help us.

Hymn

At the third hour your faithful band
Was clothed with power on Pentecost.
Bestow your Spirit on us now,
And give us strength to do your will.

Psalm 119:105-108

Your word is a lantern to my feet *
    and a light upon my path.

I have sworn and am determined *
    to keep your righteous judgments.

I am deeply troubled; *
    preserve my life, O LORD, according to your word.

Accept, O LORD, the willing tribute of my lips, *
    and teach me your judgments.

Lesson

God's love has been poured into our hearts
through the Holy Spirit that has been given to us.
Romans 5:5

⊕ The Lord's Prayer

Our Father, who art in heaven,
hallowed be thy Name,
thy kingdom come,
thy will be done,
on earth as it is in heaven.
Give us this day our daily bread.
And forgive us our trespasses,
as we forgive those
who trespass against us.
And lead us not into temptation,
but deliver us from evil.
For thine is the kingdom,
and the power, and the glory,
for ever and ever. Amen.

Thanksgiving

We thank you also for those disappointments and
failures that lead us to acknowledge our dependence
on you alone.

Grace

Let us bless the Lord.
Thanks be to God.

Wednesday
EVENING

Opening Sentence

Yours is the day, O God, yours also the night; you established the moon and the sun. You fixed all the boundaries of the earth; you made both summer and winter. *Psalm 74:15-16*

Canticle — *The Song of Mary*

My soul proclaims the greatness of the Lord,
my spirit rejoices in God my Savior; *
    for he has looked with favor on his lowly servant.
From this day all generations will call me blessed: *
    the Almighty has done great things for me,
    and holy is his Name.
He has mercy on those who fear him *
    in every generation.
He has shown the strength of his arm, *
    he has scattered the proud in their conceit.
He has cast down the mighty from their thrones, *
    and has lifted up the lowly.
He has filled the hungry with good things, *
    and the rich he has sent away empty.

He has come to the help of his servant Israel, *
    for he has remembered his promise of mercy,
The promise he made to our fathers, *
    to Abraham and his children for ever.

*Glory to the Father, and to the Son, and to the Holy Spirit: *
    as it was in the beginning, is now, and will be for ever.*
                                                    Amen.

Psalm 137:1-6

By the waters of Babylon we sat down and wept, *
    when we remembered you, O Zion.

As for our harps, we hung them up *
    on the trees in the midst of that land.

For those who led us away captive asked
                                    us for a song,
and our oppressors called for mirth: *
    "Sing us one of the songs of Zion."

How shall we sing the LORD's song *
    upon an alien soil?

If I forget you, O Jerusalem, *
    let my right hand forget its skill.

Let my tongue cleave to the roof of my mouth
if I do not remember you, *
    if I do not set Jerusalem above my highest joy.

Lesson

Do you not know that in a race the runners all compete, but only one receives the prize? Run in such a way that you may win it. *1 Corinthians 9:24*

✤ The Lord's Prayer

Our Father, who art in heaven,
hallowed be thy Name,
thy kingdom come,
thy will be done,
on earth as it is in heaven.
Give us this day our daily bread.
And forgive us our trespasses,
as we forgive those
who trespass against us.
And lead us not into temptation,
but deliver us from evil.
For thine is the kingdom,
and the power, and the glory,
for ever and ever. Amen.

Collect

O God, the life of all who live, the light of the faithful, the strength of those who labor, and the repose of the dead: We thank you for the blessings of the day that is past, and humbly ask for your protection through the coming night. Bring us in safety to the morning hours; through him who died and rose again for us, your Son our Savior Jesus Christ. *Amen.*

Grace

The grace of our Lord Jesus Christ, and the love of God, and the fellowship of the Holy Spirit, be with us all evermore. *Amen.*

COMPLINE

Opening Sentence

The Lord Almighty grant us a peaceful night and a perfect end. *Amen.*

Psalm 134

Behold now, bless the LORD, all you servants
of the LORD,
you that stand by night in the house of the LORD.

Lift up your hands in the holy place and
bless the LORD; *
the LORD who made heaven and earth bless you
out of Zion.

Lesson

Discipline yourselves, keep alert. Like a roaring lion
your adversary the devil prowls around, looking for
someone to devour. Resist him, steadfast in your
faith. *1 Peter 5:8-9a*

✤ The Lord's Prayer

Our Father, who art in heaven,
hallowed be thy Name,
thy kingdom come,
thy will be done,
on earth as it is in heaven.
Give us this day our daily bread.
And forgive us our trespasses,
as we forgive those
who trespass against us.
And lead us not into temptation,
but deliver us from evil.
For thine is the kingdom,
and the power, and the glory,
for ever and ever. Amen.

Collect

Visit this place, O Lord, and drive far from it all snares of the enemy; let your holy angels dwell with us to preserve us in peace; and let your blessing be upon us always; through Jesus Christ our Lord. *Amen.*

Antiphon

Guide us waking, O Lord, and guard us sleeping; that awake we may watch with Christ, and asleep we may rest in peace.

Canticle — *The Song of Simeon*

Lord, you now have set your servant free *
    to go in peace as you have promised;
For these eyes of mine have seen the Savior, *
    whom you have prepared for all the world to see:
A Light to enlighten the nations, *
    and the glory of your people Israel.

*Glory to the Father, and to the Son, and to the Holy Spirit: *
    as it was in the beginning, is now, and will be for ever.*
                      Amen.

Antiphon

Guide us waking, O Lord, and guard us sleeping;
that awake we may watch with Christ, and asleep
we may rest in peace.

Grace

The almighty and merciful Lord, Father, Son, and
Holy Spirit, bless us and keep us. *Amen.*

Thursday

Thursday

MORENG

Opening Sentence

All we like sheep have gone astray; we have turned every one to his own way; and the Lord has laid on him the iniquity of us all. *Isaiah 53:6*

Canticle — *The Third Song of Isaiah*

Arise, shine, for your light has come, *
    and the glory of the Lord has dawned upon you.
For behold, darkness covers the land; *
    deep gloom enshrouds the peoples.
But over you the Lord will rise, *
    and his glory will appear upon you.
Nations will stream to your light, *
    and kings to the brightness of your dawning.
Your gates will always be open; *
    by day or night they will never be shut.
They will call you, The City of the Lord, *
    The Zion of the Holy One of Israel.
Violence will no more be heard in your land, *
    ruin or destruction within your borders.
You will call your walls, Salvation, *
    and all your portals, Praise.
The sun will no more be your light by day; *

by night you will not need the brightness
of the moon.
The Lord will be your everlasting light, *
and your God will be your glory.

*Glory to the Father, and to the Son, and to the Holy Spirit: **
as it was in the beginning, is now, and will be for ever.
Amen.

Psalm 8

O Lord our Governor, *
how exalted is your Name in all the world!

Out of the mouths of infants and children *
your majesty is praised above the heavens.

You have set up a stronghold against your adversaries,*
to quell the enemy and the avenger.

When I consider your heavens, the work of your fingers, *
the moon and the stars you have set in their courses,

What is man that you should be mindful of him? *
the son of man that you should seek him out?

You have made him but little lower than the angels;*
you adorn him with glory and honor;

You give him mastery over the works of your hands;*
you put all things under his feet:

All sheep and oxen, *
even the wild beasts of the field,

The birds of the air, the fish of the sea, *
   and whatsoever walks in the paths of the sea.

O LORD our Governor, *
   how exalted is your Name in all the world!

Lesson

For the grace of God has appeared, bringing salvation
to all, training us to renounce impiety and worldly
passions, and in the present age to live lives that are
self-controlled, upright, and godly. *Titus 2:11-12*

✠ The Lord's Prayer

Our Father, who art in heaven,
   hallowed be thy Name,
   thy kingdom come,
   thy will be done,
      on earth as it is in heaven.
Give us this day our daily bread.
And forgive us our trespasses,
   as we forgive those
      who trespass against us.
And lead us not into temptation,
   but deliver us from evil.
For thine is the kingdom,
   and the power, and the glory,
   for ever and ever. Amen.

Collect

Heavenly Father, in you we live and move and have our being: We humbly pray you so to guide and govern us by your Holy Spirit, that in all the cares and occupations of our life we may not forget you, but may remember that we are ever walking in your sight; through Jesus Christ our Lord. *Amen.*

Grace

May the God of hope fill us with all joy and peace in believing through the power of the Holy Spirit. *Amen.*

NOON

Opening Sentence

O God, make speed to save us.
O Lord, make haste to help us.

Hymn

O God, creation's ruling force,
O Jesus, crucified for us,
O Spirit, love's life-giving ray,
We praise and bless you every hour.

Psalm 121

I lift up my eyes to the hills; *
    from where is my help to come?

My help comes from the LORD, *
    the maker of heaven and earth.

He will not let your foot be moved *
    and he who watches over you will not fall asleep.

Behold, he who keeps watch over Israel *
    shall neither slumber nor sleep;

The LORD himself watches over you; *
    the LORD is your shade at your right hand,

So that the sun shall not strike you by day, *
    nor the moon by night.

The LORD shall preserve you from all evil; *
    it is he who shall keep you safe.

The LORD shall watch over your going out and
                    your coming in, *
    from this time forth for evermore.

Lesson

So if anyone is in Christ, there is a new creation: everything old has passed away; see, everything has become new! All this is from God, who reconciled us to himself through Christ, and has given us the ministry of reconciliation. *2 Corinthians 5:17-18*

 # The Lord's Prayer

Our Father, who art in heaven,
hallowed be thy Name,
thy kingdom come,
thy will be done,
on earth as it is in heaven.
Give us this day our daily bread.
And forgive us our trespasses,
as we forgive those
who trespass against us.
And lead us not into temptation,
but deliver us from evil.
For thine is the kingdom,
and the power, and the glory,
for ever and ever. Amen.

Thanksgiving

Above all, we thank you for your Son Jesus Christ; for the truth of his Word and the example of his life; for his steadfast obedience, by which he overcame

temptation; for his dying, through which he overcame death; and for his rising to life again, in which
we are raised to the life of your kingdom.

Grace
Let us bless the Lord.
Thanks be to God.

EVENING

Opening Sentence
If I say, "Surely the darkness will cover me, and
the light around me turn to night," darkness is
not dark to you, O Lord; the night is as bright as
the day; darkness and light to you are both alike.
Psalm 139:10-11

Canticle — *The Song of Mary*
My soul proclaims the greatness of the Lord,
my spirit rejoices in God my Savior; *
    for he has looked with favor on his lowly servant.
From this day all generations will call me blessed: *
    the Almighty has done great things for me,
    and holy is his Name.

He has mercy on those who fear him *
    in every generation.
He has shown the strength of his arm, *
    he has scattered the proud in their conceit.
He has cast down the mighty from their thrones, *
    and has lifted up the lowly.
He has filled the hungry with good things, *
    and the rich he has sent away empty.
He has come to the help of his servant Israel, *
    for he has remembered his promise of mercy,
The promise he made to our fathers, *
    to Abraham and his children for ever.

*Glory to the Father, and to the Son, and to the Holy Spirit: *
    as it was in the beginning, is now, and will be for ever.*
                                                    Amen.

Psalm 61

Hear my cry, O God, *
    and listen to my prayer.

I call upon you from the ends of the earth
with heaviness in my heart; *
    set me upon the rock that is higher than I.

For you have been my refuge, *
    a strong tower against the enemy.

I will dwell in your house for ever; *
    I will take refuge under the cover of your wings.

For you, O God, have heard my vows; *
 you have granted me the heritage of those who
   fear your Name.

Add length of days to the king's life; *
 let his years extend over many generations.

Let him sit enthroned before God for ever; *
 bid love and faithfulness watch over him.

So will I always sing the praise of your Name, *
 and day by day I will fulfill my vows.

Lesson

But in fact Christ has been raised from the dead, the
first fruits of those who have died. For since death
came through a human being, the resurrection of the
dead has also come through a human being; for as
all die in Adam, so all will be made alive in Christ.
1 Corinthians 15:20-22

 # The Lord's Prayer

Our Father, who art in heaven,
 hallowed be thy Name,
 thy kingdom come,
 thy will be done,
   on earth as it is in heaven.
 Give us this day our daily bread.
 And forgive us our trespasses,
  as we forgive those

who trespass against us.
And lead us not into temptation,
but deliver us from evil.
For thine is the kingdom,
and the power, and the glory,
for ever and ever. Amen.

Collect

Lord Jesus, stay with us, for evening is at hand and
the day is past; be our companion in the way, kindle
our hearts, and awaken hope, that we may know you
as you are revealed in Scripture and the breaking of
bread. Grant this for the sake of your love. *Amen.*

Grace

May the God of hope fill us with all joy and peace
in believing through the power of the Holy Spirit.
Amen.

COMPLINE

Opening Sentence

The Lord Almighty grant us a peaceful night and a
perfect end. *Amen.*

Psalm 4

Answer me when I call, O God, defender of
                    my cause; *
    you set me free when I am hard-pressed;
    have mercy on me and hear my prayer.

"You mortals, how long will you dishonor my glory?*
    how long will you worship dumb idols
    and run after false gods?"

Know that the LORD does wonders for the faithful; *
    when I call upon the LORD, he will hear me.

Tremble, then, and do not sin; *
    speak to your heart in silence upon your bed.

Offer the appointed sacrifices *
    and put your trust in the LORD.

Many are saying,
"Oh, that we might see better times!" *
    Lift up the light of your countenance upon us,
                    O LORD.

You have put gladness in my heart, *
    more than when grain and wine and oil increase.

I lie down in peace; at once I fall asleep; *
    for only you, LORD, make me dwell in safety.

Lesson

Yet you, O LORD, are in the midst of us, and we are
called by your name; do not forsake us! *Jeremiah 14:9*

The Lord's Prayer

Our Father, who art in heaven,
hallowed be thy Name,
thy kingdom come,
thy will be done,
on earth as it is in heaven.
Give us this day our daily bread.
And forgive us our trespasses,
as we forgive those
who trespass against us.
And lead us not into temptation,
but deliver us from evil.
For thine is the kingdom,
and the power, and the glory,
for ever and ever. Amen.

Collect

Keep watch, dear Lord, with those who work, or
watch, or weep this night, and give your angels charge
over those who sleep. Tend the sick, Lord Christ; give
rest to the weary, bless the dying, soothe the suffering,
pity the afflicted, shield the joyous; and all for your
love's sake. *Amen.*

Antiphon

Guide us waking, O Lord, and guard us sleeping;
that awake we may watch with Christ, and asleep
we may rest in peace.

Canticle — *The Song of Simeon*

Lord, you now have set your servant free *
    to go in peace as you have promised;
For these eyes of mine have seen the Savior, *
    whom you have prepared for all the world to see:
A Light to enlighten the nations, *
    and the glory of your people Israel.

*Glory to the Father, and to the Son, and to the Holy Spirit: **
    as it was in the beginning, is now, and will be for ever.
                        Amen.

Antiphon

Guide us waking, O Lord, and guard us sleeping;
that awake we may watch with Christ, and asleep
we may rest in peace.

Grace

The almighty and merciful Lord, Father, Son, and
Holy Spirit, bless us and keep us. *Amen.*

Friday

Friday

MORMING

Opening Sentence

Let the words of my mouth and the meditation of my heart be acceptable in your sight, O Lord, my strength and my redeemer. *Psalm 19:14*

Canticle — *A Song to the Lamb*

Splendor and honor and kingly power *
    are yours by right, O Lord our God,
For you created everything that is, *
    and by your will they were created and have
                    their being;

And yours by right, O Lamb that was slain, *
    for with your blood you have redeemed for God,
From every family, language, people, and nation, *
    a kingdom of priests to serve our God.

And so, to him who sits upon the throne, *
    and to Christ the Lamb,
Be worship and praise, and dominion and splendor,*
    for ever and for evermore.

Glory to the Father, and to the Son, and to the Holy Spirit: *
as it was in the beginning, is now, and will be for ever.
Amen.

Psalm 51:1-18

Have mercy on me, O God, according to your
loving-kindness; *
in your great compassion blot out my offenses.

Wash me through and through from my wickedness*
and cleanse me from my sin.

For I know my transgressions, *
and my sin is ever before me.

Against you only have I sinned *
and done what is evil in your sight.

And so you are justified when you speak *
and upright in your judgment.

Indeed, I have been wicked from my birth, *
a sinner from my mother's womb.

For behold, you look for truth deep within me, *
and will make me understand wisdom secretly.

Purge me from my sin, and I shall be pure; *
wash me, and I shall be clean indeed.

Make me hear of joy and gladness, *
that the body you have broken may rejoice.

Hide your face from my sins *
  and blot out all my iniquities.

Create in me a clean heart, O God, *
  and renew a right spirit within me.

Cast me not away from your presence *
  and take not your holy Spirit from me.

Give me the joy of your saving help again *
  and sustain me with your bountiful Spirit.

I shall teach your ways to the wicked, *
  and sinners shall return to you.

Deliver me from death, O God, *
  and my tongue shall sing of your righteousness,
  O God of my salvation.

Open my lips, O Lord, *
  and my mouth shall proclaim your praise.

Had you desired it, I would have offered sacrifice,*
  but you take no delight in burnt-offerings.

The sacrifice of God is a troubled spirit *
  a broken and contrite heart, O God, you will
                    not despise.

Lesson

And being found in human form, he humbled
himself and became obedient to the point of
death—even death on a cross. Therefore God also

highly exalted him and gave him the name that is above every name, so that at the name of Jesus every knee should bend, in heaven and on earth and under the earth, and every tongue should confess that Jesus Christ is Lord, to the glory of God the Father.
Philippians 2:7-11

✤ The Lord's Prayer

Our Father, who art in heaven,
hallowed be thy Name,
thy kingdom come,
thy will be done,
on earth as it is in heaven.
Give us this day our daily bread.
And forgive us our trespasses,
as we forgive those
who trespass against us.
And lead us not into temptation,
but deliver us from evil.
For thine is the kingdom,
and the power, and the glory,
for ever and ever. Amen.

Collect

Almighty God, whose most dear Son went not up to joy but first he suffered pain, and entered not into glory before he was crucified: Mercifully grant that we, walking in the way of the cross, may find it none other than the way of life and peace; through Jesus Christ your Son our Lord. *Amen.*

Grace

Glory to God whose power, working in us, can do infinitely more than we can ask or imagine: Glory to him from generation to generation in the Church, and in Christ Jesus for ever and ever. *Amen.*

NOON

Opening Sentence

O God, make speed to save us.
O Lord, make haste to help us.

Hymn

Grant us, when this short life is past,
The glorious evening that shall last;
That, by a holy death attained,
Eternal glory may be gained.

Psalm 126

When the LORD restored the fortunes of Zion, *
    then were we like those who dream.

Then was our mouth filled with laughter, *
    and our tongue with shouts of joy.

Then they said among the nations, *
    "The LORD has done great things for them."

The Lord has done great things for us, *
    and we are glad indeed.

Restore our fortunes, O LORD, *
    like the watercourses of the Negev.

Those who sowed with tears *
    will reap with songs of joy.

Those who go out weeping, carrying the seed, *
    will come again with joy, shouldering their sheaves.

Lesson

For from the rising of the sun to its setting my name
is great among the nations, and in every place incense
is offered to my name, and a pure offering; for my
name is great among the nations, says the LORD of
hosts. *Malachi 1:11*

# The Lord's Prayer

Our Father, who art in heaven,
hallowed be thy Name,
thy kingdom come,
thy will be done,
on earth as it is in heaven.
Give us this day our daily bread.
And forgive us our trespasses,
as we forgive those
who trespass against us.
And lead us not into temptation,
but deliver us from evil.
For thine is the kingdom
and the power, and the glory,
for ever and ever. Amen.

Thanksgiving

Grant us the gift of your Spirit, that we may know Christ and make him known; and through him, at all times and in all places, may give thanks to you in all things. *Amen.*

Grace

Let us bless the Lord.
Thanks be to God.

EVENING

Opening Sentence

Night after night, I have set the LORD always before me. *Psalm 16:7-8*

Canticle — *The Song of Mary*

My soul proclaims the greatness of the Lord,
my spirit rejoices in God my Savior; *
    for he has looked with favor on his lowly servant.
From this day all generations will call me blessed: *
    the Almighty has done great things for me,
    and holy is his Name.
He has mercy on those who fear him *
    in every generation.
He has shown the strength of his arm, *
    he has scattered the proud in their conceit.
He has cast down the mighty from their thrones, *
    and has lifted up the lowly.
He has filled the hungry with good things, *
    and the rich he has sent away empty.
He has come to the help of his servant Israel, *
    for he has remembered his promise of mercy,
The promise he made to our fathers, *
    to Abraham and his children for ever.

*Glory to the Father, and to the Son, and to the Holy Spirit: *
as it was in the beginning, is now, and will be for ever.*
Amen.

Psalm 116

I love the LORD, because he has heard the voice of
my supplication, *
    because he has inclined his ear to me whenever I
    called upon him.

The cords of death entangled me; *
the grip of the grave took hold of me;
    I came to grief and sorrow.

Then I called upon the Name of the LORD: *
"O LORD, I pray you, save my life."

Gracious is the LORD and righteous; *
    our God is full of compassion.

The LORD watches over the innocent; *
    I was brought very low, and he helped me.

Turn again to your rest, O my soul, *
    for the LORD has treated you well.

For you have rescued my life from death, *
    my eyes from tears, and my feet from stumbling.

I will walk in the presence of the LORD *
    in the land of the living.

I believed, even when I said,
"I have been brought very low." *
　　In my distress I said, "No one can be trusted."

How shall I repay the LORD *
　　for all the good things he has done for me?

I will lift up the cup of salvation *
　　and call upon the Name of the LORD.

I will fulfill my vows to the LORD *
　　in the presence of all his people.

Precious in the sight of the LORD *
　　is the death of his servants.

O LORD, I am your servant; *
　　I am your servant and the child of your handmaid;
　　you have freed me from my bonds.

I will offer you the sacrifice of thanksgiving *
　　and call upon the Name of the LORD.

I will fulfill my vows to the LORD *
　　in the presence of all his people.

In the courts of the LORD's house, *
　　in the midst of you, O Jerusalem.
　　Hallelujah!

Lesson

And whatever you do, in word or deed, do everything in the name of the Lord Jesus, giving thanks to God the Father through him. *Colossians 3:17*

⊕ The Lord's Prayer

Our Father, who art in heaven,
  hallowed be thy Name,
  thy kingdom come,
  thy will be done,
    on earth as it is in heaven.
Give us this day our daily bread.
And forgive us our trespasses,
  as we forgive those
    who trespass against us.
And lead us not into temptation,
  but deliver us from evil.
For thine is the kingdom,
  and the power, and the glory,
  for ever and ever. Amen.

Collect

Lord Jesus Christ, by your death you took away the sting of death: Grant to us your servants so to follow in faith where you have led the way, that we may at length fall asleep peacefully in you and wake up in your likeness; for your tender mercies' sake. *Amen.*

Grace

May the God of hope fill us with all joy and peace in believing through the power of the Holy Spirit. *Amen.*

Friday

COMPLINE

Opening Sentence

The Lord Almighty grant us a peaceful night and a perfect end. *Amen.*

Psalm 31

In you, O Lord, have I taken refuge;
let me never be put to shame: *
    deliver me in your righteousness.

Incline your ear to me; *
    make haste to deliver me.

Be my strong rock, a castle to keep me safe,
for you are my crag and my stronghold; *
    for the sake of your Name, lead me and guide me.

Take me out of the net that they have secretly set
for me, *
for you are my tower of strength.

Into your hands I commend my spirit, *
for you have redeemed me,
O LORD, O God of truth.

Lesson

"Come to me, all you that are weary and carrying
heavy burdens, and I will give you rest. Take my
yoke upon you, and learn from me; for I am gentle
and humble in heart, and you will find rest for your
souls. For my yoke is easy, and my burden is light."
Matthew 11:28-30

The Lord's Prayer

Our Father, who art in heaven,
hallowed be thy Name,
thy kingdom come,
thy will be done,
on earth as it is in heaven.
Give us this day our daily bread.
And forgive us our trespasses,
as we forgive those
who trespass against us.

And lead us not into temptation,
  but deliver us from evil.
For thine is the kingdom,
  and the power, and the glory,
  for ever and ever. Amen.

Collect

O God, your unfailing providence sustains the world we live in and the life we live: Watch over those, both night and day, who work while others sleep, and grant that we may never forget that our common life depends upon each other's toil; through Jesus Christ our Lord. *Amen.*

Antiphon

Guide us waking, O Lord, and guard us sleeping; that awake we may watch with Christ, and asleep we may rest in peace.

Canticle — *The Song of Simeon*

Lord, you now have set your servant free *
  to go in peace as you have promised;
For these eyes of mine have seen the Savior, *
  whom you have prepared for all the world to see:
A Light to enlighten the nations, *
  and the glory of your people Israel.

*Glory to the Father, and to the Son, and to the Holy Spirit: ***
as it was in the beginning, is now, and will be for ever.
Amen.

Antiphon

Guide us waking, O Lord, and guard us sleeping; that awake we may watch with Christ, and asleep we may rest in peace.

Grace

The almighty and merciful Lord, Father, Son, and Holy Spirit, bless us and keep us. *Amen.*

Saturday

Saturday
MORNING

Opening Sentence

Grace to you, and peace from God our Father and
the Lord Jesus Christ. *Philippians 1:2*

Canticle — *The Song of the Redeemed*

O ruler of the universe, Lord God,
great deeds are they that you have done, *
   surpassing human understanding.
Your ways are ways of righteousness and truth, *
   O King of all the ages.
Who can fail to do you homage, Lord,
and sing the praises of your Name? *
   for you only are the Holy One.
All nations will draw near and fall down before you,*
   because your just and holy works have been
            revealed.

*Glory to the Father, and to the Son, and to the Holy Spirit: *
   as it was in the beginning, is now, and will be for ever.*
                      Amen.

Psalm 42

As the deer longs for the water-brooks, *
  so longs my soul for you, O God.

My soul is athirst for God, athirst for the living God;*
  when shall I come to appear before the presence
      of God?

My tears have been my food day and night, *
  while all day long they say to me,
  "Where now is your God?"

I pour out my soul when I think on these things: *
  how I went with the multitude and led them
            into the house of God,

With the voice of praise and thanksgiving, *
  among those who keep holy-day.

Why are you so full of heaviness, O my soul? *
  and why are you so disquieted within me?

Put your trust in God; *
  for I will yet give thanks to him,
  who is the help of my countenance, and my God.

My soul is heavy within me; *
  therefore I will remember you from the land of
      Jordan,
  and from the peak of Mizar among the heights
      of Hermon.

One deep calls to another in the noise of your
                    cataracts; *
    all your rapids and floods have gone over me.

The LORD grants his loving-kindness in the
                    daytime; *
    in the night season his song is with me,
    a prayer to the God of my life.

I will say to the God of my strength,
"Why have you forgotten me? *
    and why do I go so heavily while the enemy
                    oppresses me?"

While my bones are being broken, *
    my enemies mock me to my face;

All day long they mock me *
    and say to me, "Where now is your God?"

Why are you so full of heaviness, O my soul? *
    and why are you so disquieted within me?

Put your trust in God; *
    for I will yet give thanks to him,
    who is the help of my countenance, and my God.

Lesson

Love is patient; love is kind; love is not envious or
boastful or arrogant or rude. It does not insist on its
own way; it is not irritable or resentful; it does not
rejoice in wrongdoing, but rejoices in the truth. It

bears all things, believes all things, hopes all things, endures all things. *1 Corinthians 13:4-7*

✤ The Lord's Prayer

Our Father, who art in heaven,
hallowed be thy Name,
thy kingdom come,
thy will be done,
on earth as it is in heaven.
Give us this day our daily bread.
And forgive us our trespasses,
as we forgive those
who trespass against us.
And lead us not into temptation,
but deliver us from evil.
For thine is the kingdom,
and the power, and the glory,
for ever and ever. Amen.

Collect

Almighty God, who after the creation of the world rested from all your works and sanctified a day of rest for all your creatures: Grant that we, putting away all earthly anxieties, may be duly prepared for the service of your sanctuary, and that our rest here upon earth may be a preparation for the eternal rest promised to your people in heaven; through Jesus Christ our Lord. *Amen.*

Grace

The grace of our Lord Jesus Christ, and the love of God, and the fellowship of the Holy Spirit, be with us all evermore. *Amen.*

NOON

Opening Sentence

O God, make speed to save us.
O Lord, make haste to help us.

Hymn

Almighty Father, hear our cry
Through Jesus Christ, our Lord Most High,
Whom with the Spirit we adore
For ever and for ever more.

Psalm 119:105-108

Your word is a lantern to my feet *
 and a light upon my path.

I have sworn and am determined *
 to keep your righteous judgments.

I am deeply troubled; *

    preserve my life, O Lᴏʀᴅ, according to your word.

Accept, O Lᴏʀᴅ, the willing tribute of my lips, *

    and teach me your judgments.

Lesson

God's love has been poured into our hearts through the Holy Spirit that has been given to us. *Romans 5:5*

✤ The Lord's Prayer

Our Father, who art in heaven,
    hallowed be thy Name,
    thy kingdom come,
    thy will be done,
        on earth as it is in heaven.
Give us this day our daily bread.
And forgive us our trespasses,
    as we forgive those
        who trespass against us.
And lead us not into temptation,
    but deliver us from evil.
For thine is the kingdom,
    and the power, and the glory,
    for ever and ever. Amen.

Thanksgiving

Accept, O Lord, our thanks and praise for all that you have done for us. We thank you for the splendor of the whole creation, for the beauty of this world, for the wonder of life, and for the mystery of love.

Grace

Let us bless the Lord.
Thanks be to God.

Saturday

EVENING

Opening Sentence

Jesus said, "I am the light of the world; whoever follows me will not walk in darkness, but will have the light of life." *John 8:12*

Canticle — *The Song of Mary*

My soul proclaims the greatness of the Lord,
my spirit rejoices in God my Savior; *
    for he has looked with favor on his lowly servant.

From this day all generations will call me blessed: *
    the Almighty has done great things for me,
    and holy is his Name.
He has mercy on those who fear him *
    in every generation.
He has shown the strength of his arm, *
    he has scattered the proud in their conceit.
He has cast down the mighty from their thrones, *
    and has lifted up the lowly.
He has filled the hungry with good things, *
    and the rich he has sent away empty.
He has come to the help of his servant Israel, *
    for he has remembered his promise of mercy,
The promise he made to our fathers, *
    to Abraham and his children for ever.

*Glory to the Father, and to the Son, and to the Holy Spirit: *
    as it was in the beginning, is now, and will be for ever.*
                                        Amen.

Psalm 15

LORD, who may dwell in your tabernacle? *
    who may abide upon your holy hill?

Whoever leads a blameless life and does what is right,*
    who speaks the truth from his heart.

There is no guile upon his tongue;
he does no evil to his friend; *
    he does not heap contempt upon his neighbor.

In his sight the wicked is rejected, *
    but he honors those who fear the LORD.

He has sworn to do no wrong *
    and does not take back his word.

He does not give his money in hope of gain, *
    nor does he take a bribe against the innocent.

Whoever does these things *
    shall never be overthrown.

Lesson

Whoever speaks must do so as one speaking the very words of God; whoever serves must do so with the strength that God supplies, so that God may be glorified in all things through Jesus Christ. To him belong the glory and the power forever and ever. Amen. *1 Peter 4:11*

✤ The Lord's Prayer

Our Father, who art in heaven,
    hallowed be thy Name,
    thy kingdom come,
    thy will be done,
        on earth as it is in heaven.
Give us this day our daily bread.
And forgive us our trespasses,
    as we forgive those
        who trespass against us.

> *And lead us not into temptation,*
> *but deliver us from evil.*
> *For thine is the kingdom,*
> *and the power, and the glory,*
> *for ever and ever.* Amen.

Collect

O God, the source of eternal light: Shed forth your unending day upon us who watch for you, that our lips may praise you, our lives may bless you, and our worship on the morrow give you glory; through Jesus Christ our Lord. *Amen.*

Grace

The grace of our Lord Jesus Christ, and the love of God, and the fellowship of the Holy Spirit, be with us all evermore. *Amen.*

COMPLINE

Opening Sentence

The Lord Almighty grant us a peaceful night and a perfect end. *Amen.*

Psalm 134

Behold now, bless the LORD, all you servants of
                        the LORD, *
    you that stand by night in the house of the LORD.

Lift up your hands in the holy place and bless
                        the LORD; *
    the LORD who made heaven and earth
                        bless you out of Zion.

Lesson

Discipline yourselves, keep alert. Like a roaring lion
your adversary the devil prowls around, looking for
someone to devour. Resist him, steadfast in your
faith. *1 Peter 5:8-9a*

✠ The Lord's Prayer

Our Father, who art in heaven,
*   hallowed be thy Name,*
*   thy kingdom come,*
*   thy will be done,*
*   on earth as it is in heaven.*
Give us this day our daily bread.
And forgive us our trespasses,
*   as we forgive those*
*   who trespass against us.*

And lead us not into temptation,
but deliver us from evil.
For thine is the kingdom,
and the power, and the glory,
for ever and ever. Amen.

Collect

We give you thanks, O God, for revealing your Son Jesus Christ to us by the light of his resurrection: Grant that as we sing your glory at the close of this day, our joy may abound in the morning as we celebrate the Paschal mystery; through Jesus Christ our Lord. *Amen.*

Antiphon

Guide us waking, O Lord, and guard us sleeping; that awake we may watch with Christ, and asleep we may rest in peace.

Canticle — *The Song of Simeon*

Lord, you now have set your servant free *
    to go in peace as you have promised;
For these eyes of mine have seen the Savior, *
    whom you have prepared for all the world to see:
A Light to enlighten the nations, *
    and the glory of your people Israel.

Glory to the Father, and to the Son, and to the Holy Spirit: *
as it was in the beginning, is now, and will be for ever.
Amen.

Antiphon

Guide us waking, O Lord, and guard us sleeping;
that awake we may watch with Christ, and asleep
we may rest in peace.

Grace

The almighty and merciful Lord, Father, Son, and
Holy Spirit, bless us and keep us. *Amen.*

Prayers

Seasonal Prayers

ADVENT

Almighty God, give us grace to cast away the works of darkness, and put on the armor of light, now in the time of this mortal life in which your Son Jesus Christ came to visit us in great humility; that in the last day, when he shall come again in his glorious majesty to judge both the living and the dead, we may rise to the life immortal; through him who lives and reigns with you and the Holy Spirit, one God, now and for ever. *Amen.*

CHRISTMAS

O God, you make us glad with the yearly festival of the birth of your only Son Jesus Christ: Grant that we, who joyfully receive him as our Redeemer, may with sure confidence behold him when he comes to be our Judge; who lives and reigns with you and the Holy Spirit, one God, now and for ever. *Amen.*

EPIPHANY

O God, by the leading of a star you manifested your only Son to the peoples of the earth: Lead us, who know you now by faith, to your presence, where we may see your glory face to face; through Jesus Christ our Lord, who lives and reigns with you and the Holy Spirit, one God, now and for ever. *Amen.*

LENT

Almighty and everlasting God, you hate nothing you have made and forgive the sins of all who are penitent: Create and make in us new and contrite hearts, that we, worthily lamenting our sins and acknowledging our wretchedness, may obtain of you, the God of all mercy, perfect remission and forgiveness; through Jesus Christ our Lord, who lives and reigns with you and the Holy Spirit, one God, for ever and ever. *Amen.*

HOLY WEEK

Almighty God, whose most dear Son went not up to joy but first he suffered pain, and entered not into glory before he was crucified: Mercifully grant that we, walking in the way of the cross, may find it none other than the way of life and peace; through Jesus Christ your Son our Lord, who lives and reigns with you and the Holy Spirit, one God, for ever and ever. *Amen.*

MAUNDY THURSDAY

Almighty Father, whose dear Son, on the night before he suffered, instituted the Sacrament of his Body and Blood: Mercifully grant that we may receive it thankfully in remembrance of Jesus Christ our Lord, who in these holy mysteries gives us a pledge of eternal life; and who now lives and reigns with you and the Holy Spirit, one God, for ever and ever. *Amen.*

GOOD FRIDAY

Almighty God, we pray you graciously to behold this your family, for whom our Lord Jesus Christ was willing to be betrayed, and given into the hands of sinners, and to suffer death upon the cross; who now lives and reigns with you and the Holy Spirit, one God, for ever and ever. *Amen.*

HOLY SATURDAY

O God, Creator of heaven and earth: Grant that, as the crucified body of your dear Son was laid in the tomb and rested on this holy Sabbath, so we may await with him the coming of the third day, and rise with him to newness of life; who now lives and reigns with you and the Holy Spirit, one God, for ever and ever. *Amen.*

EASTER

O God, who for our redemption gave your only-begotten Son to the death of the cross, and by his glorious resurrection delivered us from the power of our enemy: Grant us so to die daily to sin, that we may evermore live with him in the joy of his resurrection; through Jesus Christ your Son our Lord, who lives and reigns with you and the Holy Spirit, one God, now and for ever. *Amen.*

ASCENSION

Almighty God, whose blessed Son our Savior Jesus Christ ascended far above all heavens that he might fill all things: Mercifully give us faith to perceive that, according to his promise, he abides with his Church on earth, even to the end of the ages; through Jesus Christ our Lord, who lives and reigns with you and the Holy Spirit, one God, in glory everlasting. *Amen.*

PENTECOST

Almighty God, on this day you opened the way of eternal life to every race and nation by the promised gift of your Holy Spirit: Shed abroad this gift throughout the world by the preaching of the Gospel, that it may reach to the ends of the earth;

through Jesus Christ our Lord, who lives and reigns with you, in the unity of the Holy Spirit, one God, for ever and ever. *Amen.*

TRINITY SUNDAY

Almighty and everlasting God, you have given to us your servants grace, by the confession of a true faith, to acknowledge the glory of the eternal Trinity, and in the power of your divine Majesty to worship the Unity: Keep us steadfast in this faith and worship, and bring us at last to see you in your one and eternal glory, O Father; who with the Son and the Holy Spirit live and reign, one God, for ever and ever. *Amen.*

ALL SAINTS

Almighty God, you have knit together your elect in one communion and fellowship in the mystical body of your Son Christ our Lord: Give us grace so to follow your blessed saints in all virtuous and godly living, that we may come to those ineffable joys that you have prepared for those who truly love you; through Jesus Christ our Lord, who with you and the Holy Spirit lives and reigns, one God, in glory everlasting. *Amen.*

Occasional Prayers

BAPTISM

We thank you, Almighty God, for the gift of water. Over it the Holy Spirit moved in the beginning of creation. Through it you led the children of Israel out of their bondage in Egypt into the land of promise. In it your Son Jesus received the baptism of John and was anointed by the Holy Spirit as the Messiah, the Christ, to lead us, through his death and resurrection, from the bondage of sin into everlasting life. *Amen.*

We thank you, Father, for the water of Baptism. In it we are buried with Christ in his death. By it we share in his resurrection. Through it we are reborn by the Holy Spirit. Therefore in joyful obedience to your Son we bring into his fellowship those who come to him in faith, baptizing them in the Name of the Father, and of the Son, and of the Holy Spirit. *Amen.*

CONFIRMATION

Grant, Almighty God, that we, who have been redeemed from the old life of sin by our baptism into the death and resurrection of your Son Jesus Christ, may be renewed in your Holy Spirit, and live in righteousness and true holiness; through Jesus Christ our Lord, who lives and reigns with you and the Holy Sprit, one God, now and for ever. *Amen.*

MARRIAGE

O gracious and everliving God, you have created us male and female in your image: Look mercifully upon this man and this woman who come to you seeking your blessing, and assist them with your grace, that with true fidelity and steadfast love they may honor and keep the promises and vows they make; through Jesus Christ our Savior, who lives and reigns with you in the unity of the Holy Spirit, one God, for ever and ever. *Amen.*

O God, you have so consecrated the covenant of marriage that in it is represented the spiritual unity between Christ and his Church: Send therefore your blessing upon these your servants, that they may so love, honor and cherish each other in faithfulness and patience, in wisdom and true godliness, that their home may be a haven of blessing and peace; through Jesus Christ our Lord, who lives and reigns with you and the Holy Spirit, one God, now and for ever. *Amen.*

Almighty God, giver of life and love, bless *N.* and *N.* Grant them wisdom and devotion in the ordering of their common life, that each may be to the other a strength in need, a counselor in perplexity, a comfort in sorrow, and a companion in joy. And so knit their wills together in your will, and their spirits in your

Spirit, that they may live together in love and peace all the days of their life; through Jesus Christ our Lord. *Amen.*

CHILDBIRTH

O God, you have taught us through your blessed Son that whoever receives a little child in the name of Christ receives Christ himself: We give you thanks for the blessing you have bestowed upon this family in giving them a child. Confirm their joy by a lively sense of your presence with them, and give them calm strength and patient wisdom as they seek to bring this child to love all that is true and noble, just and pure, lovable and gracious, excellent and admirable, following the example of our Lord and Savior, Jesus Christ. *Amen.*

RECONCILIATION

Have mercy on me, O God, according to your loving-kindness; in your great compassion blot out my offenses. Wash me through and through from my wickedness, and cleanse me from my sin. For I know my transgressions only too well, and my sin is ever before me. Holy God, Holy and Mighty, Holy Immortal One, have mercy upon us. Pray for me, a sinner. *Amen.*

SICKNESS

This is another day, O Lord. I know not what it will bring forth, but make me ready, Lord, for whatever it may be. If I am to stand up, help me to stand bravely. If I am to sit still, help me to sit quietly. If I am to lie low, help me to do it patiently. And if I am to do nothing, let me do it gallantly. Make these words more than words, and give me the Spirit of Jesus. *Amen.*

O God, the source of all health: So fill my heart with faith in your love, that with calm expectancy I may make room for your power to possess me, and gracefully accept your healing; through Jesus Christ our Lord. *Amen.*

O heavenly Father, you give your children sleep for the refreshing of soul and body: Grant me this gift, I pray; keep me in that perfect peace which you have promised to those whose minds are fixed on you; and give me such a sense of your presence, that in the hours of silence I may enjoy the blessed assurance of your love; through Jesus Christ our Lord. *Amen.*

DEATH

Depart, O Christian soul, out of this world; In the Name of God the Father Almighty who created you; In the Name of Jesus Christ who redeemed you; In the Name of the Holy Spirit who sanctifies you. May your rest be this day in peace, and your dwelling place in the Paradise of God. *Amen.*

Into your hands, O merciful Savior, we commend your servant *N.* Acknowledge, we humbly beseech you, a sheep of your own fold, a lamb of your own flock, a sinner of your own redeeming. Receive *him/her* into the arms of your mercy, into the blessed rest of everlasting peace, and into the glorious company of the saints in light. *Amen.*

GRIEF

Grant, O Lord, to all who are bereaved the spirit of faith and courage, that they may have the strength to meet the days to come with steadfastness and patience; not sorrowing as those without hope, but in thankful remembrance of your great goodness, and in the joyful expectation of eternal life with those they love. And this we ask in the Name of Jesus Christ our Savior. *Amen.*

Familiar Prayers

PEACE — *Attributed to St. Francis*

Lord, make us instruments of your peace. Where
there is hatred, let us sow love; where there is injury,
pardon; where there is discord, union; where there
is doubt, faith; where there is despair, hope; where
there is darkness, light; where there is sadness, joy.
Grant that we may not so much seek to be consoled
as to console; to be understood as to understand; to
be loved as to love. For it is in giving that we receive;
it is in pardoning that we are pardoned; and it is in
dying that we are born to eternal life. *Amen.*

LONELINESS

Keep watch, dear Lord, with those who work, or
watch, or weep, and give your angels charge over
those who sleep. Tend the sick, Lord Christ; give rest
to the weary, bless the dying, soothe the suffering,
pity the afflicted, shield the joyous; and all for your
love's sake. *Amen.*

QUIET CONFIDENCE

O God of peace, who has taught us that in returning
and rest we shall be saved, in quietness and in
confidence shall be our strength: By the might of

your Spirit, lift us, we pray, to your presence, where we may be still and know that you are God; through Jesus Christ our Lord. *Amen.*

DIRECTION

O God, because without you, we are not able to please you, mercifully grant that your Holy Spirit may in all things direct and rule our hearts; through Jesus Christ our Lord, who lives and reigns with you and the Holy Spirit, one God, now and for ever. *Amen.*

Direct us, O Lord, in all our doings with your most gracious favor, and further us with your continual help; that in all our works begun, continued, and ended in you, we may glorify your holy Name, and finally, by your mercy, obtain everlasting life; through Jesus Christ our Lord. *Amen.*

O God, by whom the meek are guided in judgment, and light rises up in darkness for the godly: Grant us, in all our doubts and uncertainties, the grace to ask what you would have us to do, that the Spirit of wisdom may save us from all false choices, and that in your light we may see light, and in your straight path may not stumble; through Jesus Christ our Lord. *Amen.*

COMFORT

God, grant me the serenity to accept the things I cannot change, courage to change the things I can, and wisdom to know the difference. *Amen.*

ENEMIES

O God, the Father of all, whose Son commanded us to love our enemies: Lead them and us from prejudice to truth; deliver them and us from hatred, cruelty, and revenge; and in your good time enable us all to stand reconciled before you; through Jesus Christ our Lord. *Amen.*

FAMILIES

Almighty God, our heavenly Father, who sets the solitary in families: We commend to your continual care the homes in which your people dwell. Put far from them, we beseech you, every root of bitterness, the desire of vainglory, and the pride of life. Fill them with faith, virtue, knowledge, temperance, patience, godliness. Knit together in constant affection those who, in holy wedlock, have been made one flesh. Turn the hearts of the parents to the children, and the hearts of the children to the parents; and so enkindle fervent charity among us all, that we may evermore be kindly affectioned one to another; through Jesus Christ our Lord. *Amen.*

THANKSGIVING

Accept, O Lord, our thanks and praise for all that you have done for us. We thank you for the splendor of the whole creation, for the beauty of this world, for the wonder of life, and for the mystery of love.

We thank you for the blessing of family and friends, and for the loving care which surrounds us on every side.

We thank you for setting us at tasks which demand our best efforts, and for leading us to accomplishments which satisfy and delight us.

We thank you also for those disappointments and failures that lead us to acknowledge our dependence on you alone.

Above all, we thank you for your Son Jesus Christ; for the truth of his Word and the example of his life; for his steadfast obedience, by which he overcame temptation; for his dying, through which he overcame death; and for his rising to life again, in which we are raised to the life of your kingdom.

Grant us the gift of your Spirit, that we may know Christ and make him known; and through him, at all times and in all places, may give thanks to you in all things. *Amen.*